Write and
Get PAID!

Gregory Lovvorn

DEDICATION

To my wonderful wife who believed in me and my ability long
before I did. You're still the best idea I ever had.

Thank you

CONTENTS

ACKNOWLEDGMENTS

This book and indeed my writing career would not of been possible without the help and guidance of many friends. I can't list them all but they should know who they are.

1 INTRODUCTION

I am not a person that has been writing for years. I do not have a degree in journalism, English, or creative writing. My degrees are in engineering and environmental fields. I have only been writing professionally for approximately six months and from what I have been told I am doing a very good job and making much more than I should be at this point.

In six months I have gone from a novice, writer want-a-be, to supporting my family solely on my writing income. I won't tell you it has been easy, or ever will be, but it can be done and I want to share my story with you and tell you how you can do it too.

2 MY STORY

June 12, 2012 is the day that changed my life forever, I was working in Kuwait as a military contractor and life was pretty good. My wife and I had a nice apartment, I enjoyed my job, and the money was nice. It wasn't a life for everyone but for me it was a great fit. Then I had an on the job accident and destroyed my right leg from the knee down.

I had a class three tear of my Achilles Tendon, tore the heads out of two of my three right calf muscles and broke my heal. The doctors said I would, at best be on crutches or a cane for the rest of my life, all I could tell them is "you don't know me".

Months of hospital time and therapy did get me back to just using a cane but that was the good part of the story. The bad part was that while I was out on temporary disability, my company went through a downsizing and guess who, the first person they cut was, me. I don't blame them I was deadwood on the books.

Being out of work, in Kuwait, means you no longer have a Visa and must vacate the country. For tax reasons I choose to move to the Philippines rather than return to the United States. My wife and I took the little savings that we had and moved to the land of ocean breezes and eternal summer.

Things were good for a few months, we had money in the bank and after 3 years of sand and dust, the green of the Philippines was a welcome change. Unfortunately money in the bank quickly disappears if you have no income coming in. We were slowly going broke and trust me the Philippines is not a country to be broke in. I needed to find work so I started looking for the same types of jobs I had worked in the past Environmental, Water, and Waste Water.

It quickly became obvious, that there wasn't much out there. The economy in the states was terrible and overseas my age (48) was playing against me along with my injury. I was walking unaided but still had a pronounced limp. I told you, the doctors didn't know me. While I was looking our savings continued to dribble away.

I was spending 10 to 12 hours a day online looking for work and not getting anywhere. I must have sent out at least 1000 resumes but had no takers. I am very lucky man that my wife, ever supportive, rather than running me down, asked me one day. Why don't you try writing on line, you told me you dreamed of being a writer, when you were young, now is your chance to try. I was skeptical but desperate so I took her words as a personal challenge and started looking for ways to make money writing online.

The rest as they say is history. I have now had over 400 articles published. Some under my own name which means residual income but the majority under someone else's name, I have written copy for uncounted web sites, and catalogues. I have been published in e-zines and have my own food blog. I work through several content websites and am considered a top writer at some. It is very gratifying when clients start requesting you over the other writers on a site, especially when, as I said, I have never been formally trained as a writer.

How have I accomplished this? That is what I will share along the way as you read further. My lack of formal training has enabled me to stretch and grow in directions that better equipped writers may not have been able to. Here I will begin to teach you my (the Lovvorn) writing for profit method.

3 WRITE, READ, AND STUDY

There are three things that you must begin to do if you want to be a successful writer. The first is obvious, you have to write. You have to write as much as can, as often as you can, and about as many different subjects as you can. We will discuss how to write a little later.

I started out with the idea of having a Food Blog and I still have my blog it has just now after months of work started to make any kind of income. It was not my best choice for starting a writing career. Making money as Blogger takes time and dedication to your blog.

Success as a blogger is as much about promotion, networking, and monetization as it is about writing. You have to provide excellent quality articles but will find you spend as much or more time promoting your site and chatting with other bloggers in an attempt to build an audience as you will spend writing and the monetary return is slow in coming. I was ignorant but don't want you to be, so I'm telling you, wait about starting a blog. They eat a lot of time and energy.

A better choice for starting your writing career is a site like Bubblews (http://www.bubblews.com/?referral=511f38c7c1bca8.97981584) where you can write and post almost anything from what you had for breakfast to a dissertation on moon rocks. The limits on this site are simple. All work has to original (no plagiarism) and all post must be 400 characters. No that is not a typo it is 400 characters not 400 words.

This is a great site to break in on as you can post as much as you want. The pay can be a little haphazard but you can make money on this site and you will be a part of one of the most supportive communities on the web. A writer writes and this site gives you the chance to do just that and will teach you to self-edit as it doesn't have anyone to do it for you.

If you do decide to try Bubblews the key to making money is to make connections. In the beginning make as many connections as you can. They will become your audience and the key to profiting from this site. It is also very beneficial to join a support group. I would recommend one Facebook group in particular. It is Bubblews approved and will support you no matter where you write or blog. The admins are excellent and very supportive. You can find it at https://www.facebook.com/groups/bloggingtogether/ . This is one of the best groups I know of and it has helped my growth immensely.

The second thing you need to do if you want to grow as a writer is to read. This may seem a little odd but it is one of the most important things a writer can do. Whatever style of writing you chose to enter you need to read the top writers in that field. By reading you will accomplish two things one you will relax your mind. This is more paramount than you will realize until you crank out several thousand words a day for a week or so and hit your burn-out point. Your brain needs a break and reading will give it a chance to unwind and settle down.

The other thing reading accomplishes is that you will be learning while your relaxing. It doesn't matter who or what you read you will subconsciously be learning from the author. Your brain will automatically absorb style, rhythm, and syntax without you having to go through the rigors of studying. This process is completely natural and you will be surprised how much reading good writers on regular bases will influence and improve your own voice.

The last thing you have to do and it pains me to say this, you have to study. There are certain things you are going to be expected to know as a writer. You will be expected to know the different voices (first person, second person, third person) and how to use them. You will be expected to know and understand the AP style book, it is the industry standard for most writing sites and probable most important if you're going to make money writing online you need to understand SEO (search engine optimization) and how it can work for you.

I have articles that make money for me month after month, without any further work on my part, because I did an excellent job with my keyword research and other SEO practices. Needless to say they are my favorite pieces and my future retirement income.

Don't worry if you don't know all the technical jargon (that's what Google define is for) or think that you have got to spend money to learn these things, there are many free resources available that will teach you what you need to know. I started learning when I picked a second site to write for, Yahoo Contributor Network (http://contributor.yahoo.com/join//?refer=1721243). Yahoo has a free Writers Academy that is more than worthwhile to go through. It will teach you about AP style, SEO, how to promote and so much more. It is taught in individual modules, written in everyday words so that even the tech challenged, like myself, can understand it.

After the first level (it has three levels) of the Academy you can start submitting articles. That's right, at YCN you have to submit your articles for review and trust me it can be shocking the first time you get a rejection notice. Work with the editors though, they are not your enemy, and they will help you learn how to be a better web writer where you can build that residual income I was talking about earlier.

When you submit to YCN you will have to choose what rights you want to retain and whither you want upfront payment, view pay or just to post and have your work seen. My recommendation is to always submit for upfront payment in the non-exclusive rights section. Later we will talk more about publishing rights but for right now just remember you never give up rights you don't have to. Restructuring an article for reuse is part of making money as a writer but if you give someone exclusive rights to your work and use a rewrite somewhere else, it is called plagiarism and copyright infringement, even if you are the original writer.

4 MY NEXT STEP

Writing for Yahoo was very gratifying in many ways. They taught me a lot of things that have served me well and I still write for them from time to time. It is a good place to build a following and they allow me add links to my other writings, in my articles, so I build cross traffic from them but it would be almost impossible to make a living just with YCN. Besides as Warren Buffet says, never put all your eggs in one basket.

I soon realized that I was building a fair collection of articles that were good articles but for one reason or another weren't right for yahoo. I hate waste and anything that I have taken time to research and write but haven't published is a waste. This led me to look for other places to publish my work. I was completely shocked when I found out how many places there were to publish online.

Many of these offer income sharing from your articles some offer one time payments and some both. You will have to look at these and decide what you want to accomplish and which sites best fit your particular areas of interest. I have written and still do for a couple of these sites. I'll list below a few of the more reputable sites, that I have worked with, but this list is far from exhaustive better I tell you to Google the phrase "profit sharing writing sites" and see what pops up. Trust me you will be aghast at the number of returns you will get. A few word of caution here, not all sites are reputable. Do your homework, before you waste quality content on a site that doesn't pay, as promised and some sites insist on you giving them exclusive and enduring rights to your work, I personally avoid these like the plague. My right to reuse my research and rewrite my content is part of the way I survive as a writer.

Profit, Revenue Sharing sites:

Triond (www.triond.com) One of the first revenue split sites that I worked for and still one of my favorites. The revenue is not the highest out there but if you are good at selecting subjects and doing your keyword research, you can make a little money. The two biggest things in favor of this site are that they pay like clock-work and the editors are very helpful and easy to work with.

Hubpages (hubpages.com) - Hubpages is one of the more popular sites for beginner writers and can be quite profitable. They offer one unique feature in that if you have an Adsense account or are part of the Ebay and Amazon affiliate programs you can place your own links and increase you revenue. This means four income streams from one source.

Experts Pages (expertspages.com) - Another very reputable site that has never failed to make sure that I had my money when I was supposed to. Pick a subject that you have knowledge of and start making money. One of the things I really like about Expert pages is they seem to base earnings on page views not just click through rates. For a writer that can generate an audience but isn't a salesman this is a big advantage.

Helium (www.helium.com) - "Where knowledge is king" is their motto and they mean it. You can write on almost any subject that you have knowledge of or are willing to gain knowledge of. For this site you will need to sharpen your research skills but as a writer that is a good thing.

As I said this is just a spattering of the sites that are out there for you choose from. A complete list of all the available sites would be a volume all by itself and new ones are popping up every day. Again I want to caution you to do your due diligence before submitting your work to any site. Make sure they are reputable and be sure to read (as boring as they can be) the terms of service and contract sections before signing up at any site.

5 ARTICLE MILLS

Article or content mills are some of my favorite sites and where I generate most of my income. There are literally thousands of people out there needing content written and many if not most of them turn to these sites. You can find work writing product descriptions, webpage content, blogs, product reviews, e-books, and almost any other kind of work you can imagine. That is one of the things I enjoy most about these sites. I never know what I am going to write next. It depends on my mood and who is asking for what content at what price.

The way these sites function is they get an order from a client. The client will ask for a certain word count, of a certain type (blog, product description, etc.) on a particular subject, by a certain time. The site will post it on an order board along with what the job will pay (flat rate or by word) and you pick what you want to write. Write the requested content and submit it.

There is usually some provision made for reviews and rewrites and this process varies a great deal from site but once the content is accepted you get paid. The vast majority of times, these sites, pay through PayPal making it quick and easy to get your money.

Most of these sites pay you by the word with a very wide range of payment being offered. I have written for as little as .005 cents a word and have been paid as much as 1.70 a word. For most of these sites you will have to qualify as a writer. This may involve something as simple as submitting a writing sample or it may involve taking several test and several samples of different types of writing to qualify. As a general rule the harder the site is to qualify with the better they pay. Don't expect to make big money out of the gate with any of them. Regardless of how good your test scores or your writing samples you will have to earn your strips. Be patient, do good work, never miss a deadline and you will quickly move up. The key, as with any business, is happy clients.

You keep your clients happy and you will soon be getting, direct request for your work. Direct orders mean one; you can stop watching the job boards and two, the customer and the site pay premium prices.

It is not unusual for me to make several hundred dollars a week from a single site, working basically when I want and writing what I choose.

Here is a list of my favorite Content Mills:

Crowed Content (www.crowdcontent.com) is a fairly young website but it is quickly making a name for itself. The big plus here is it pays every other Friday and even with holidays they are never late. The pay rates are higher than some sites and lower than others but they offer a bonus system based on your order Turnaround Time (TAT). If you can research and write your articles quickly, the income from Crowd Content can be very nice.

Text Broker (www.textbroker.com) could be called one of the granddaddies of this type of site. It is one of the oldest and busiest sites out there. The pay is moderate to low but the variety and volume of work out they list makes up for the pay. They also have team projects that pay very well. I defiantly recommend you find a good team and join it. Another great thing about this site is the editors truly seem to care about the writers and there craft. Every piece you submit is reviewed and you will receive a critique and suggestions on how to improve. For young writers this can be a critical feature.

Text Broker UK (www.textbroker.co.uk) is the British sister site to Text Broker and operates exactly the same with one added bonus, they pay in Euros. This may seem like a small difference but when you check the exchange rates it can make a big difference in your actual income.

Cloud Crowd (www.cloudcrowd.com/i/6wtgg5) is one of the hardest sites to qualify for. As a writer, you can expect to spend several days just getting accepted, but it is worth the effort. It not only has some of the highest pay rates out there it has special sections devoted to marketing writers, technical writers and legal writers. You can also find plenty of work here as an editor. This is great for those times when you just don't feel like writing but still need to make money and best of all Cloud Crowd pays daily.

These are just my four favorite sites at the moment, as with the income sharing sites new ones come along on a daily bases and I am always looking for a site that pays a little better. My Grandfather taught me "pennies make dollars" and when you're getting paid by the word the pennies add up fast.

6 MAKE A BID AND SEE WHAT HAPPENS

Once I had worked my way up on the content mills to a point where I felt comfortable not just with my writing skills but also with my ability to support a few luxuries like water and electricity I started looking for writing jobs that offered a little more security. A friend and fellow writer suggested that I should look at some of the freelancing contract sites. She told me that she and her husband (a web designer) were working almost exclusively through these sites. Never afraid to try something new, I gave them a look and liked what I found.

On these sites, people post all kinds of jobs. About any kind of work that can be done from home can be found on them. The basic mechanics of these sites is pretty much universal. People post their needs. You read the ads and if you choose make a bid. You set your own price, you set your own milestones and the site adds a percentage that they will receive. For me, the advantage of these sites is you can find longer term projects that can also led to referral business.

It is more than possible to start a small company, either like my friend, whose husband has skills that compliment her own or by yourself as a writer. The biding is highly competitive on many of these sites but once you build a reputation you can find yourself being sought after rather than always chasing the next deal. If you do good work and keep your customers happy you may find yourself hiring other people to help with the work load. At that point you can quite calling yourself a writer and start calling yourself an entrepreneur.

Taking that step is strictly a matter of personal choice. My friend loves being the business woman, I prefer to stay independent and just worry about my writing. For her, her business is now writing, for me, my writing is my business. It is just a different mindset.

Either one you chose, as long as it makes you happy, is the right choice. I will only offer two suggestions for this type of site. I like these two because they offer a lot of flexibility and they both give you ratings on the people asking for bids. As with every category not everyone is reliable and it can be comforting to know the person you're contracting with has a good track record of paying on time and being easy to work with.

Elancer (www.elance.com) has a great variety of jobs and contest available. Your bids are highly customizable and they offer time tracking to keep everyone involved honest.

Freelancer (www.freelancer.com) my favorite of all these sites. If you can think of a feature you would to see on a freelance contract site you will more than likely find it here and the support is outstanding.

There are other sites out there, Odesk is one very popular site, but I hesitate to recommend it as I have had issues with clients there and I can't recommend any of the others as I have had little to no personal experience working with them. Again as always do your due diligent research on any site you choose to work with.

7 NOT THE END

There you have my story, as a writer. In Six short months, I have recreated myself and built a new career, doing something that I love. If you notice, no where do I claim to be a good much less a great writer. I know my mechanics are weak and I'm working on that, just I am still working on improving all my skills.

For me writing is a labor of love that it just happens I have a slight talent for. I have been truly blessed in this journey in having the support of a wonderful woman as well as many good friends. There is nothing magical about my journey other than the fact that I am slowly succeeding.

I said at the beginning of this book that it has been hard work and it has. Some days I have written 5000+ plus words and spent over 12 hours at the keyboard. I had no choice. I had bills to pay. Has the work been worth it? Yes, every second and every word has been worthwhile.

My purpose in writing this has not been to teach you how to be a writer but to show you it can be done and hopefully convey a little information that might be of assistance in helping you reach your writing dreams.

The biggest lesson I hope that everyone who reads this will take away is that you should never give up or be satisfied. Necessity caused me to keep looking for a better place to publish, another place to learn and a way to make my writing pay a little more.

If I can succeed, so can you, just don't give up on your dream and never, ever, for any reason Quite.

I would love to hear from you. Please share your thoughts and suggestions with me at Glovvornblog@gmail.com.

8 12 SUGGESTED WRITING SITES

Yahoo Contributor Network-
http://contributor.yahoo.com/join//?refer=1721243

Triond- http://www.triond.com

 Hubpages- http://hubpages.com

Experts Pages- http://expertspages.com

Helium- http://www.helium.com

Crowed Content- http://www.crowdcontent.com

Text Broker- http://www.textbroker.com

Text Broker UK- http://www.textbroker.co.uk

Cloud Crowd- http://www.cloudcrowd.com/i/6wtgg5

Elancer- http://www.elance.com

Freelancer- http://www.freelancer.com

ABOUT THE AUTHOR

Father of six, Grandfather of two, Gregg recreated himself as a writer at the age of 48. His former life was spent in the environmental work which allowed him to travel the world and absorb many different cultures.

Proudly American but considering himself a citizen of the world Gregory now lives in the Philippines with his wife Dang, their dog Kali Wali (Arabic for it doesn't matter)and an ever flowing group of family and friends.

"It is better to live than survive" and "Grow or die" are the two quotes that most exemplify Gregg's outlook on life. A lifetime student with unlimited curiosity his interest include fields as varied as organic gardening and Business Management.

A voracious reader and writer Gregg has authored over 100 articles under his own name and over 300 as a ghost writer.